Milky's Way

at the

Zoo

Story by

Valerie Miele

Illustrations by
Peter J. Bergamo Jr.

Dedicated to my son, Lucas

Each day a tiny snow white kitten named Milky would walk through the zoo.

She'd walk past the lions and would admire their magnificent manes. Their manes looked so majestic as they blew in the wind. Oh how she longed for a mane like that.

She'd walk past the zebras and would
admire their beautiful stripes. They
were so pretty basking in the sun.
Oh how she longed for stripes like that.

She'd walk past the tigers and would admire their voice. They were so loud when they would yell to the others. Oh how she longed to have a voice like that.

She'd walk past the bears and would admire
their size and strength. They were so tall and
strong when they stood on two feet.
Oh how she longed to be tall like that.

She'd walk past the cheetahs and would admire their speed. They were so fast when they would race across the field. Oh how she longed to be fast like that.

One day Milky decided she wanted a mane like a lion, stripes like a zebra, a voice like a tiger, height like a bear, and speed like a cheetah. So...

She gathered leaves and scattered them around
her face so she could have a mane like a lion.

And she painted black stripes all over so she could be beautiful like a zebra.

She made a microphone out of old newspapers
so she could have a voice like a tiger.

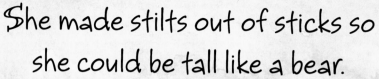
She made stilts out of sticks so she could be tall like a bear.

18

She put roller blades on her feet so
she could be fast like a cheetah.

She walked past a window and saw her reflection. She looked silly. She looked nothing like a lion or a bear. Nor did she look like a tiger or a cheetah or a zebra.

She didn't understand, she had a mane like a lion, height like a bear, a voice like a tiger, speed like a cheetah, and stripes like a zebra but she was still not happy with the way she looked.

It began to rain and the stripes slowly washed away. As the wind blew the leaves around her face fluttered away, the stick stilts rolled away along with the paper microphone and the roller blades. All that was left was a tiny snow white kitten.

A little boy passed by, seeing the cute kitten he stopped. As he picked up Milky, he softly said, "Aw you poor kitty, your beautiful fur is getting wet."

Milky sadly replied, "I'm not beautiful. I don't have a beautiful mane or stripes. I'm not tall, fast, or loud. I have nothing."

The little boy just smiled and said, "But I like you the way you are."

25

That night Milky purred contently on the little boy's bed. She no longer had dreams of being anything else but herself.

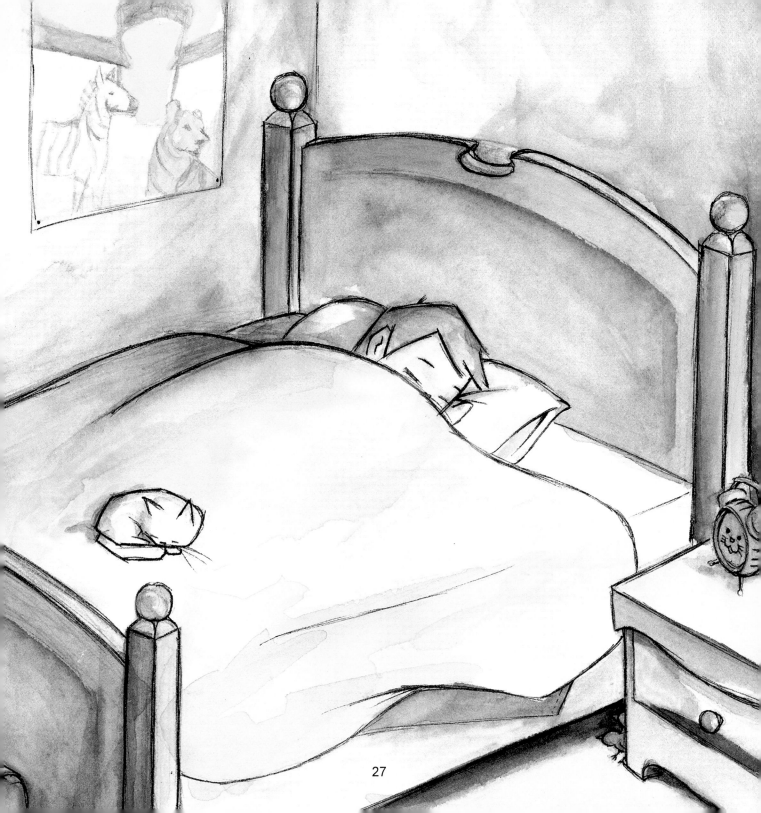

To order additional copies of this book, contact:
Xlibris LLC
1-888-795-4274
www.Xlibris.com
Orders@Xlibris.com

Edwards Brothers Malloy
Thorofare, NJ USA
September 9, 2014